A Note to Parents and Teachers

DK READERS is a compelling reading programme for children, designed in conjunction with leading literacy experts, including Cliff Moon M.Ed., Honorary Fellow of the University

cher and
ten more
editor

graphs
fresh
DER is
ing his
eading.

rent
at

The "normal" age at which a child begins to read can be anywhere from three to eight years old. Adult participation through the lower levels is very helpful for providing encouragement, discussing storylines and sounding out unfamiliar words.

No matter which level you select, you can be sure that you are helping your child learn to read, then read to learn!

Sch

Production Georgina Hayworth
DTP Designer Ben Hung
Jacket Designer Mary Sandberg

Reading Consultant
Cliff Moon, M.Ed.

Published in Great Britain by
Dorling Kindersley Limited
80 Strand, London WC2R 0RL

Copyright © 2007 Dorling Kindersley Limited
A Penguin Company

2 4 6 8 10 9 7 5 3 1
DD407 - 04/07

ISBN: 978-1-4053-2167-9

Colour reproduction by Colourscan, Singapore
Printed and bound in China by L Rex Printing Co., Ltd.

The publisher would like to thank the following for their kind
permission
to reproduce their photographs:
(Key: a-above; b-below/bottom; c-centre; l-left; r-right; t-top)

Alamy Images: Available Light Photography 31b; David R. Frazier
Photolibrary, Inc. 8-9; Justin Kase 30b; Motoring Picture Library /
National Motor Museum 6t; Greg Randles 16-17; Robert Harding
Picture Library Ltd 10-11; Trevor Smithers ARPS 24-25t; Alan Stone
12-13; Mel Stuart 20t; vario images GmbH & Co.KG 4-5, 31t;
BAE Systems 2007 : 26tl, 26-27t; **Corbis**: George Hall 18-19t;
Mark M. Lawrence 29t; Gary I Rothstein / epa 28t; David Sailors
7t; Terraqua Images 22-23cb; Ronald Wittek / dpa 30t; **DK Images**:
Judith Miller / Wallis And Wallis 27bl (grey submarine); National
Maritime Museum, London 25bl (trawler); **Ford Motor Company
Ltd**: 3b, 6bl, 7bl, 7br; **Getty Images**: Lori Adamski Peek 14t; Jim
Cummins 15; Ed Darack 22t; Richard Price 21t

All other images © Dorling Kindersley
For further information see: www.dkimages.com

Discover more at
www.dk.com

Contents

On the Move

A Dorling Kindersley Book

There are many ways to travel.

Cars go on the roads.
Broom!
Off they go.

windscreen

 cars

Lorries rumble along the roads.
They carry heavy loads.

load

 lorries

cab

Trains move fast along the railway tracks.

engine

trains

They whizz past.

carriage

Tractors drive on farms.
They go up and down
the fields.

cab

tractors

wheel

Bikes go along the paths.
Their wheels go round
and round.

bikes

helmet

wheel

15

Buses go along the streets.
People get on and off.

 buses

light

SCHOOL BUS

wing

Planes fly in the sky.
Zoom! Off they go.

planes

engine

Hot-air balloons float
in the sky.
They go up, up and away!

basket / \ burner

hot-air balloons

Helicopters whirr
through the air.
Their blades spin around.

6684

helicopters

blade

Boats sail on the water.
They cut through
the waves.

boats

flag

wave

25

submarines

Submarines glide
through the sea.
They dive under the water.

Space shuttles zoom
off into space.
Whoosh! Off they go!

launch pad

space shuttles

We can travel by air . . .

by road . . .

by rail . . .

or by sea.

Which way do you like best?

Glossary

Bike a vehicle with two wheels

Bus a road vehicle that travels along a fixed route

Helicopter an aircraft with spinning blades

Space shuttle a flying vehicle that travels into space and back again

Tractor a four-wheeled farm vehicle